✳ Animal Rescue ✳

CHIMP RESCUE

Clare Hibbert

LIBRARIES NI
WITHDRAWN FROM STOCK

W
FRANKLIN WATTS
LONDON•SYDNEY

D0311994

First published in 2015 by Franklin Watts

Copyright © Arcturus Holdings Limited

Franklin Watts
338 Euston Road
London
NW1 3BH

Franklin Watts Australia
Level 17/207 Kent Street, Sydney, NSW 2000

Produced by Arcturus Publishing Limited,
26/27 Bickels Yard, 151–153 Bermondsey
Street, London SE1 3HA

All rights reserved.

Editor: Joe Harris
Picture researcher: Clare Hibbert
Designer: Tokiko Morishima

Picture credits:
All interior images supplied by Suzi Eszterhas/
Nature Picture Library, unless otherwise
specified. Karl Ammann/Nature PL: 26, 27;
Mark Carwardine/Nature PL: 6, 8–9; Fiona
Möllers/Nature PL: 24; Anup Shah: 2–3, 17,
28–29. Cover image: Suzi Eszterhas/Nature PL.

A CIP catalogue record for this book is
available from the British Library.

Dewey Decimal Classification Number:
639.9'79885

ISBN: 978 1 4451 3390 4

Franklin Watts is a division of Hachette
Children's Books, an Hachette UK company.
www.hachette.co.uk

Printed in China

SL004091UK
Supplier 03, Date 1014, Print Run 3577

CONTENTS

CHIMP SANCTUARY

Chimpanzees are great apes that live in West and Central Africa. They belong to the same family as gorillas, orang-utans and human beings. Sadly, chimps are endangered. There are fewer than 300,000 left in the wild.

Many different organisations are working to look after chimps. Some have set up safe places, called sanctuaries or refuges, where chimps are protected. There are sanctuaries in many African countries, from Guinea and Sierra Leone in the west to Uganda and Kenya in the east. The Ngamba Island Chimpanzee Sanctuary is in Uganda, East Africa. It was set up in 1998 by an organisation called Chimpanzee Trust, Uganda.

4

The Ngamba Island sanctuary is on an island in Lake Victoria, the largest lake in Africa. It is a safe home for nearly 50 orphaned and rescued chimps. These chimpanzees would not be able to look after themselves if they were returned to the 'real' wild. On Ngamba Island, however, they live a life that is close to life in the wild.

SOUTH SUDAN

KENYA

D. R. CONGO

UGANDA

Ngamba Island Chimp Sanctuary

RWANDA

Lake Victoria

TANZANIA

RESCUING CHIMPS

Chimpanzees have already disappeared from four African countries where they used to live — Gambia, Burkina Faso, Benin and Togo. They have almost vanished from other countries too. There are several reasons for this.

One problem is that chimps have lost their habitat. Large areas of their rainforest home have been cut down. The chimps are left stranded in small patches of forest. They cannot mix with other chimpanzee groups, or move to new areas to find food and water.

Chimps face other dangers too. Some are hunted for meat. Some become trapped in snares that were meant for other animals. Some catch the deadly Ebola virus, which affects apes and humans. Some are captured when they are babies to be sold as pets.

Fact File: Chimps as Pets
Baby chimps look cute! It is easy to see why some people want to keep them as pets. However, chimps grow up fast. By the age of five they are stronger than most human adults and can be aggressive. They do not make good pets at all.

NGAMBA ISLAND

Ngamba is one of a group of islands on Lake Victoria. It is fairly small, covering just over 40 hectares (100 acres). Almost all of the island is covered in tropical forest, with the odd patch of grassland.

A small fishing community used to live on Ngamba Island and those people cleared a tiny area of forest for their homes. This area is now split between the human camp and the chimps' feeding zone. There is a high walkway and viewing platform overlooking the feeding zone. The human camp is where the sanctuary's staff live and work. It is protected by an electric fence.

The only way to reach Ngamba Island is by boat from Entebbe, 23 km (14 miles) to the north, on the shore of Lake Victoria. There is no road or rail bridge and nowhere for planes to land. Visitors arrive by motorised canoe or speedboat. No one can come to the island without being noticed. This makes the sanctuary safe from poachers (hunters who kill animals illegally).

JOINING THE GROUP

Chimps are sociable animals. They live together in large groups called communities. When a new young chimp arrives on Ngamba Island, it must find its own position in the community. Ngamba is home to **47** chimps.

The alpha male is the leader of the community. If there are squabbles, he sorts them out. He's usually 20 to 26 years old, fit and strong. Next come the rest of the adult males. Their positions in the group depend on their age, fighting skills and intelligence.

This young chimp (left) has been adopted by a new mother.

Fact Files: Family Groups

Chimps in the wild live in communities of between 20 and 120 individuals. There are several generations in each group and they are all related to each other in some way. The chimps in a community live, eat, hunt and play together.

The females have their own order of importance. They are all below the males. The young chimps, below the age of 15, obey the adults. When a new infant arrives, a female chimp adopts it and helps it to settle into the community.

DINNER TIME

Chimpanzees are not fussy eaters. Most of their diet is made up of fruit but, like us humans, they are omnivores. That means they eat both plant and animal foods, although meat makes up only around two per cent of their diet.

There is an amazing variety of plants in the rainforest. Chimps look for food in small groups, picking and eating fruit, nuts, seeds, flowers, leaves and roots. Termites and other insects are on the menu too. When hunting bigger prey, the chimps use teamwork. Red colobus monkeys are a favourite. The chimps share their kill, and eat almost every part of the animal.

Avocados and other fruit for the rescue chimps.

Ngamba Island is too small to produce enough food for its community of chimps. The sanctuary carers must give the chimps extra food. Feeding time happens twice a day, at 11:00 am and 2:30 pm. Standing high on the visitor platforms, the carers offer carrots and other vegetables, plus plenty of fruit, including bananas, pineapples and avocados. All the produce comes onto the island by boat.

THE TEAM

Ngamba Island Sanctuary employs more than 20 staff. They include six carers and two vets. Whatever jobs they do, all the staff care passionately about saving chimpanzees. Staff visit from other sanctuaries for training and to learn how Ngamba Island is run.

The carers' job is to look after the chimps. They feed them twice a day and clean out their night-time cages. They also play with the young chimps and groom them. They help the animals to learn the skills they'll need as adults.

Vets give the chimps medical care. Chimps that have been rescued from traps or captivity sometimes have injuries that need treating. Some may be dehydrated (needing water) after going without drinking for some time. The chimps may also have infections or illnesses. The vets give them medicines, such as antibiotics.

Fact File: Other Staff

Some staff at the sanctuary do not work with the chimps directly, but they still do important jobs. Cooks feed the staff and visitors. The security officer and maintenance officer look after the site. Other staff work to educate visitors or local people about the sanctuary and chimp conservation.

GROOMING

Grooming means keeping fur clean and neat. By grooming themselves or each other, chimps keep their coats free of parasites. If they are lucky, they may even get a free flea snack! However, grooming also has another purpose.

When chimps groom each other, they start to build up a friendly relationship. When a chimp presents its back to another chimp for grooming, it is a sign of trust. It shows that the chimp feels safe and comfortable around the other chimp. Grooming can last for five minutes, ten minutes or even more. During that time, the animals are being calm and close to each other.

There are different grooming styles. Some animals race through the process. Others take their time and pick through the fur very slowly and carefully. Fast or slow, grooming helps the animals form relationships and it also calms troubles in the group.

HUMAN FRIENDSHIPS

The Ngamba chimps do not just form strong bonds within their chimp community. They make friends with their human carers too. They show their affection through touch, play and laughter.

Chimps are very similar to us. They use hugs to greet one another, and kisses to show affection. They like holding hands. Like us, they smile or laugh when they are feeling happy or playful. They will also cry if they feel sad or upset.

An excitable rescue chimp greets one of the keepers.

The carers know that it is not enough just to look after the chimps' basic needs, such as food and water. Chimps are complicated creatures. Like us, they need to feel close to others. The carers spend time just hanging out with the chimps, picking through their fur and relaxing.

Fact File: Feelings

Chimps show many of the emotions that we feel. They form very close relationships, just as we do with our best friends or members of our family. When chimps lose someone they love, they show grief. They comfort each other with hugs, pats and kisses.

19

PLAYTIME!

Most animals are playful when they are youngsters. Chimps remain playful even as adults. They love clowning around and having fun. They're even ticklish! Their favourite game is rough-housing — rolling around with each other and being really noisy and energetic.

At Ngamba Sanctuary, the carers are able to see the chimps' playful behaviour close up. Most of the fun and games involve the youngsters. There are wrestling matches and fast-moving chases through the trees. It is a great way for the animals to burn off energy. The carers also join in the fun when they can. It strengthens their relationships with the chimps.

Like many animals, chimps use play during childhood to practise skills they will need as adults. Play-fights and chasing make young males better at fighting, running and climbing – so they will be higher up in the community as adults. Young females practise being mums. They cradle toy sticks in their arms as if they were babies – just as human children pretend to care for dolls.

COMMUNICATION

Humans spend a lot of time talking to each other. Chimps cannot talk, but they have many different ways of communicating. They use sounds, facial expressions and body language.

Chimps have a range of different calls, each with its own meaning. A call of 'wraa,' for example, means that the chimp is afraid. 'Huu' means it is puzzled or confused. A grunt means that the chimp is enjoying its dinner! Chimps also cry and laugh.

A chimp's face can show lots of different expressions. When they want to play, they will relax their face and flop open their bottom lip to reveal their teeth. When they're scared, they will 'grin' with fear. Angry chimps, just like human toddlers, throw tantrums where they wave their arms and stamp their feet!

Fact File: Signal Sound

The 'pant-hoot' is a call chimps make when they are excited. It means, 'Here I am!' Every chimp has its own pant-hoot, unlike anyone else's. It means other chimps can tell who's calling even if the caller is out of sight.

BEDTIME

In the wild, chimps sleep in nests, which are usually in the trees. They make a fresh, new nest every evening. Sometimes they make one for their daytime nap too. Their ape cousins, gorillas and orang-utans, also make nests.

The nesting spot can be as low as 3 m (10 ft) up or as high as 145 m (475 ft). First, the chimp weaves branches together to make a platform or mattress. It tops this with a comfy layer of twigs and leaves. The finished nest is at least 5 m (16 ft) across.

On Ngamba, the chimps sometimes stay out in the forest at night and build nests like they would in the wild. Usually, though, they return to the camp instead. There are caged sleeping areas for the chimps. Before they turn in for the night, they eat a nice dish of 'posho' — warm maize porridge.

BRAINY BEHAVIOUR

Chimps are known for their intelligence. They use tools to make their lives easier. They have good memories and they can solve problems. They even make decisions — pausing and thinking about a situation before they act.

We humans may be the smartest creatures on the planet, but chimps have big brains too. Like us, they have the ability to learn, remember, make plans and use the objects around them.

Fact File: Jane Goodall
A lot of what we know about chimps was discovered by Jane Goodall, who has studied the chimps at Gombe National Park, Tanzania, for decades. She was the first to notice that chimps use tools. Jane has visited Ngamba Island several times to give talks about chimp behaviour.

One sign of chimp intelligence is their use of tools. Chimps use sticks or blades of grass to 'fish' for termites or honey. If the tool is not quite the right shape or size, they alter it so it works better. Chimps also use stone tools to crack nuts, and sticks and rocks as weapons.

REACHING OUT

The Ngamba Island Chimpanzee Sanctuary is doing an important job caring for chimps that could never live in the wild. But the island is not just a sanctuary for chimpanzees. It is also a safe home for other rare species, such as fish eagles, monitor lizards and fruit bats.

The sanctuary allows paying visitors to come to the island for the day or to stay overnight so they can see the chimps up close. As well as raising money, this helps spread the word about saving chimps. The visitors learn how important it is to protect the African rainforests where chimps live, and how terrible it is to kill chimpanzees for meat or take them as pets.

The sanctuary staff also go into schools to spread the conservation message. They help teachers to come up with ideas for lessons that will help children think more about protecting chimps and other endangered species. The staff put across their message in their online blogs too. Their writings about day-to-day life looking after the chimps are read by animal lovers all over the world.

GLOSSARY

ALPHA MALE The male leader of an animal community.

ANTIBIOTICS Substances used to treat infectious diseases because they stop bacteria from growing.

CAPTIVITY A situation where animals live with humans and are not free to return to the wild.

COMMUNITY A group of animals of the same species that live closely together.

CONSERVATION Protecting and keeping for the future.

DEHYDRATED Lacking fluids.

ENDANGERED At risk of dying out in the wild forever.

FORAGE To search for food.

GREAT APE An animal belonging to the hominid family, which includes humans, gorillas, chimpanzees and orang-utans.

HABITAT The place where an animal or plant lives.

INFANT In chimps, a youngster up to the age of five years.

INFECTION A disease or condition caused by germs such as bacteria.

OMNIVORE An animal that eats plants and animals for food.

ORPHANED Having lost its parents.

PARASITE An animal or plant that survives by living off another animal or plant.

PHYSICAL Relating to the body and its needs.

POACHER Someone who steals or kills animals illegally.

RAINFOREST A thick tropical forest where there is heavy rainfall.

SANCTUARY A safe place set up by the government or another organisation, where animals are protected from threats such as poachers and loss of habitat.

SNARE A trap for catching animals.

SPECIES A group of similar organisms that can reproduce together.

TERMITE An ant-like insect that lives in a colony that is sometimes topped by a huge mound.

FURTHER INFORMATION

WEBSITES

kids.nationalgeographic.com/animals/chimpanzee.html
Information about and photos of chimps from National Geographic.

ngambaisland.com
The website for Ngamba Island Chimpanzee Sanctuary.

www.bbc.co.uk/nature/life/Common_Chimpanzee
Information and film clips about chimps from the BBC.

www.janegoodall.org
The website of the institute Jane Goodall founded to promote the conservation of great apes; it includes lots of information about chimpanzees.

www.savethechimps.org
The website of Save the Chimps, a charity that cares for chimpanzees rescued from research laboratories, the entertainment industry and the pet trade.

FURTHER READING

100 Facts: Monkeys & Apes by Camilla de la Bedoyere (Miles Kelly Publishing, 2010)

Animal Families: Chimpanzees by Tim Harris (Wayland, 2014)

Ape by Martin Jenkins, illustrated by Vicky White (Candlewick Press, 2010)

Changing the Future for Endangered Wildlife: Chimpanzee Rescue by Patricia Bow (Firefly Books, 2004)

Discover Science: Apes and Monkeys by Barbara Taylor (Kingfisher, 2011)

My Life with the Chimpanzees by Jane Goodall (Simon & Schuster, 2007)

INDEX

* Animal Rescue *

SERIES CONTENTS

BAT HOSPITAL

Tolga Bat Hospital • Trouble with Ticks • Tick Treatment • The Nursery • Hospital Workers • Health Check • Preparing Meals • Dinner Time! • The Flight Cage • Foster Care • Return to the Wild • Dangers to Bats • Reaching Out

CHIMP RESCUE

Chimp Sanctuary • Rescuing Chimps • Ngamba Island • Joining the Group • Dinner Time • The Team • Grooming • Human Friendships • Playtime! • Communication • Bedtime • Brainy Behaviour • Reaching Out

ELEPHANT ORPHANS

Elephant Nursery • Threats to Elephants • Mother's Milk • Food Supplies • Dust Baths • A New Arrival • Health Checks • Healing Touch • Elephant Friends • Off for a Walk • Playtime • Bedtime • Spreading the Word

ORANG-UTAN ORPHANS

Saving Orang-Utans • Vanishing Forests • The Pet Trade • Mums and Babies • Carers • Dinner Time • Playtime • Bedtime • Keeping Clean • Being Friendly • Forest Skills • Back to the Wild • Spreading the Word

PANDAS IN DANGER

Panda Centres • Threats to Pandas • A Diet of Bamboo • Breeding Pandas • Newborn Pandas • Feeding Time • Growing Stronger • Better Care • Ready to Explore • Keepers • Playing Outside • Panda Society • Spreading the Word

PENGUIN RESCUE

Saving Seabirds • African Penguins • Chick Rescue • On Arrival • Daily Routine • Dinner Time • From Egg to Chick • Rearing Chicks • Chick Checks • Return to the Wild • Other Birds • Black Death • Spreading the Word